CRACKED

Paula Wells

Copyright © 2023 (Paula Wells)
All rights reserved worldwide.

No part of the book may be copied or changed in any format, sold, or used in a way other than what is outlined in this book, under any circumstances, without the prior written permission of the publisher.

Publisher: Inspiring Publishers,
P.O. Box 159, Calwell, ACT Australia 2905
Email: publishaspg@gmail.com
http://www.inspiringpublishers.com

 A catalogue record for this book is available from the National Library of Australia

National Library of Australia The Prepublication Data Service

Author: Paula Wells
Title: Cracked
Genre: Non-fiction

Paperback ISBN: 978-1-922920-87-4
eBook ISBN: 978-1-922920-89-8

1

Totally Broken

Engulfed in desperation, my mind races, obsessively rehashing the minutiae of my forthcoming actions. My heart pounds erratically, causing a sickening lurch in my stomach. Every ten minutes or so, I rush to the toilet. My palms are slick with sweat, and my entire body feels clammy. My intention is to pilfer $150 from Dad's wallet, along with his car keys. This will provide me a quarter gram of heroin and the means to procure it, guaranteeing roughly eight hours of tranquillity, escape, and stillness. I'm biding my time, waiting for the perfect moment to strike.

The truth is that I'm an addict. Physically and psychologically, I'm ensnared in heroin's unyielding grip. Once the decision to use again is made, there's no turning back until the craving is satisfied. My parents, Mum and Dad, have suffered a great deal due to my actions, and they've become adept at anticipating my next move. Wallets are kept within arm's reach throughout the day, and car keys are stashed away, usually somewhere in their bedroom.

As morning dawns, I hear the shower start, signalling Dad's pre-work routine. Mum is in the kitchen. Seizing the opportunity, I dart into their bedroom, rifling through drawers and cupboards. *Bingo!* I locate Dad's wallet and keys, grab the cash and keys, and dart out the front door. Within seconds, I'm in the car, starting it up, and beginning to reverse down the driveway. But then, *BOOM!* Dad appears, flinging himself onto the bonnet to halt my escape. A surge of fury overtakes me. Ashamedly, I contemplate fleeing, even if it means seriously injuring him, but I can't. I can't harm my beloved father, who, even at my worst, has never lost hope for me.

In that moment, I understand that I must stop. I must stop the car and this self-destructive cycle in which I'm so hopelessly ensnared. For the first time, the idea surfaces: I need to quit using heroin. Despite two stints in rehab, numerous failed attempts at getting clean, undergoing counselling, engaging with a psychologist and psychiatrist at different stages of my recovery, even resorting to acupuncture for cravings, it's this moment that brings about the stark realization: If I don't break this cycle, I'll end up alone and dying in a gutter.

For the first time in my battle with heroin addiction, I consciously choose to stop, and that, to me, means choosing life over death. Up until now, nothing else mattered beyond feeding my craving. I was a slave to the drug, trapped in a cycle of treachery and deceit.

My dad's eyes connected with mine, soul to soul, pain meeting pain, he has broken through my roller door, my shield which is what my addiction was, a place where no-one could reach me, my safety zone, and for a moment I was shocked to witness the person I had become. It was like I was witnessing myself from a higher perspective and I saw his pain, I felt his pain, I saw his desperation, I saw how crazy and desperate I was, and I knew at a very deep level that this was a life-or-death moment of decision making for me. So, I chose to live. In that moment I was enraged, I flung myself out of the car and ran to the bus stop. I was still going to score, but on the bus journey into town the magnitude of the situation dawned on me. This was my hero, my dear dad, who has only ever protected and cared for me and loved me, and I would have deliberately hurt him to get high. The glass had shattered, my fragmented fragile self was at rock bottom, and I was faced with a life-or-death choice. If I went and scored, it would be the end of me, or I could go into the methadone clinic and get signed up on the methadone program. I got off the bus in the city, went into Biala, the needle exchange centre in Brisbane, and requested to go on methadone. I had a meeting with a drug and alcohol counsellor and from there I phoned my parents to tell them what was happening and asked could I come home again. They gave me a dose of methadone to carry me through the night. As I write this now, my heart absolutely aches with the pain that I put my parents through and my behaviour at the time. All they have ever done is support and love me. I am so grateful to them, for it is with their help that I have been so successful in my recovery. At this tender point in my life, I had lost all trust and respect from Mum and Dad, and it would be a long journey over many years before I earned this back from them. I was twenty-eight years old.

2

My First Taste

I had just moved into a sharehouse with a girlfriend of mine in West End in Brisbane. It was such a find. The living space was downstairs with a fireplace, a cute kitchen and floor-to-ceiling glass windows and doors looking out onto a hidden valley of rainforest. There was a deck to step out onto, becoming immersed in nature as you did. My bedroom upstairs had its own balcony that looked out on the forest. There were people on either side but the house itself had been built so as all you could see was the forest. It was very private, and we both loved living there. My friend Elle and I both smoked pot pretty much every day. We both worked full time. She worked shift work, and I had a nine-to-five job. When we did come together there was always pot involved. Smoking pot was just a part of our lives the same way eating and drinking were. I was twenty-three years old. I had a steady boyfriend, Jed, who was a pretty nasty piece of work. He was manipulative, a gambler and an alcoholic. He was not a nice person but I was unable to see that at the time. I really admired Elle and wanted to be like her, or my perspective of her at least! She was outgoing, fun, beautiful, popular and smart. I was in a smoky dreamland living there, feeling like I was a part of something that I desired. I felt a sense of belonging. That was how I saw it at the time at any rate. I knew that Elle had used heroin in the past and I was curious about it, so it was only a matter of time before we shot up together. I must be clear here that I approached her to make it happen. It was love at first hit for me. I loved everything about it, I loved how I felt, loved the rush as the gear entered my bloodstream, loved the taboo around it, the secrecy and the dreamy wonderland it took you to. I remember we went to her friend's place to pick up the heroin and on the way, we stopped by the needle exchange to grab the equipment we needed to shoot up. It was all very new and exciting. When we had the package, Elle had said, 'Let's have it here'. And because it was my first experience with heroin, I did not understand this at the time. I swayed her into waiting till we got home (I felt safer with this option). Twelve months down the track and believe me, as soon as I had the gear I was shooting up. It didn't matter where I was, there was no waiting till I got home! Mostly it was around the corner in the car on the side of the road or in some nearby public toilet.

It wasn't just about the drug itself; there was a feeling of camaraderie, of belonging, of having an adventure together. It was an escape from my unhealthy relationship with Jed and it was stepping into a fantasy world where I felt absolute bliss. I loved that nodding-off experience, and I loved it most when I did it with others. It was a way of being social without having to engage! Perfect! Except to pass the joint or bong around, which brought on the next rush. I was in heaven! I had found my drug of choice! Who would have thought that vomiting could be so pleasurable? When you threw up, you knew you were right on the edge. If you had any more gear, then you would probably be overdosing, and you were high as a kite. Of course, that was not going to be the end of it for me.

3

The Golden Years

My next experience with heroin came about a month later, and for the initial couple of years, that was my pattern—only dabbling in heroin about once a month. I enjoyed living with Elle and occasionally indulging with her, an activity that my partner Jed was never a part of. He was firmly against heroin, and in a way, my use was a rebellion against him, something I knew he wouldn't condone.

Back then, I seldom stood up for myself and wouldn't have thought of leaving him; the idea simply didn't cross my mind. Despite fantasizing about relationships with other men to whom I was attracted, I remained with Jed due to a distorted sense of security and obligation. He was very controlling, and my heroin use was one facet of my life over which he had no control.

Elle and I kept our use a secret, occasionally including other friends from her—and eventually my—social circle. Those times were unbelievably exhilarating! We also spent considerable time partying on ecstasy, speed, or cocaine, with marijuana always in the mix. There were periods when we grew our own marijuana, and we sometimes bought and sold it just to keep our supply free.

We both managed to hold down our full-time jobs and were able to keep our work and partying lives from spilling into each other. We had six glorious months in that house and then we had to find another place to live in as the son of the owner wanted to move back in. We found another place not far from that one in Highgate Hill. It was close to the city yet had a chilled-out vibe to the suburb. This second place also had a lot of greenery around it with shrubs and trees for privacy. I was still only using once a month or so and was managing to pay my rent on time, feed myself, and be productive at work. I was selling a lot of pot at the time and every night would have people over the house. This was covering the financial cost of my marijuana addiction, but it did mean I was smoking more and more each day. I saved quite a bit of money at that time in my life. I mostly just left my wage to accumulate in my bank account and spent the drug money on living/playing expenses.

As I had started to use needles, I was regularly tested for hepatis C by my doctor. At that point, I had never shared a needle, but I did share spoons. I was misdiagnosed with the virus when I was twenty-four. I remember I was gutted at the time, thinking the worst and having no idea on how to navigate the diagnosis when a few days later my doctor appeared at our front door, which in hindsight was quite unprofessional. I invited him in, and we sat at one end of our smoke-filled lounge room with my friends and customers up the other end of the room sucking back bongs! He gave me the good news that my test results had been mixed up with someone else's and that I was not in fact hep-C positive. Phew, what a relief! Although I did end up with the disease some years later.

My love affair with the needle was beginning to develop. Whenever a group of us would be using heroin we would shuffle into a separate room of the house, a smaller space, often the bathroom or one of our bedrooms. This fostered an air of secrecy with the knowledge that what we were doing was taboo. I loved the feeling of being part of a group and living dangerously. I was twenty-four when I nearly overdosed, but it was on speed, not heroin. At this stage of my life, I was looking for any excuse to shoot up. It had been about a year since my first hit of heroin, and I was still only using drugs intravenously once a month or so. We were going to a market day in town with bands playing. I was the only one in the group taking speed. When I shot up, I had a sharp pain in my heart. I can still remember the rush as the speed hit my system. I could barely breathe, there were stars before my eyes, and a fraction more would have killed me. Nevertheless, I pulled myself together and we went out to enjoy the festivities. An hour or so later, I had to find my way into a taxi and come home. My lips had turned blue, and I could not stand upright. I had not let anyone know how serious it was for me but in hindsight I was lucky to survive. I mention this to showcase the fact that I was beginning to take big risks with no real sense of accountability in my life.

Elle and I lived in that house for a year and then she moved into her own place, and I went back to my parents' place to work out where I was going to live next. We continued to use once a month or so, usually as a group at her place. We both decided to take a trip to Thailand together. I knew that she had scored heroin there in the past and that it was a lot cheaper than in Australia and I had a mindset of making that happen on our trip. She could take it or leave it and find fun in drinking and socialising but for me it was all I could think about until we finally did score some (we had still managed to smoke pot every day there which was easy to come by). Once we had it, all I wanted to do was shoot up and smoke dope and this was the beginning of a downward spiral for me. The drug was getting its hooks in me. My mind was getting hooked. I would say that I have a strong tendency towards addiction. I have always smoked more pot than those around me. I am usually taking more of whatever drug I am on at the time than those I am using with. It takes a great deal of will for me to monitor my intake and whenever I had drugs, I was never able to have just a little and then put it aside for later. I was lucky to have not found myself in a Thai prison during that trip. On an overnight bus journey back to Bangkok, we had a stop for a toilet break. Elle and I crouched out the back of the bus which was by the main road to smoke a joint. I had about an ounce of marijuana in my backpack to keep us going until we departed for Brisbane. As we smoked the joint in the dark, sitting on the ground, a policeman walked by us. I had seen him approaching out the corner of my eye and had discreetly stubbed out the joint. I could have reached out and touched him as he walked past, casing out the place. Had he caught us in the act, things could have turned out rather differently for me. A lucky escape, I believe. It is unlikely that I would have been returning home had I been caught. I was twenty-five at the time.

On my return to Australia, I decided to move in with Jed. We found a cute little house that had been renovated with lots of stained glass throughout, a highset Queenslander with a lot of greenery around it, a bathroom housing a big claw bath with beautiful stained glass French doors opening out onto a private, leafy courtyard in East Brisbane. I loved the place and thought that I loved Jed. I did think about leaving him at times, but he would always manipulate me back into the relationship. I never had the sense of self-value that I have now.

Before heading overseas, I sold my little VW Beetle and resorted to taking the bus to the Valley for work during the week. Through my friend Elle, I had become close to Anna, a woman I greatly admired. Whenever the three of us gathered, heroin was invariably involved. Jed, my partner at the time, was oblivious to this, and I intended to keep it that way.

Increasingly, I began purchasing more heroin than necessary for the doses we three would share. Often, I would inject alone. At other times, I would invite Les, a male friend for whom I harboured feelings, and we would indulge together, often leading to intimacy. Les had a tendency to exploit whomever he could. I understood he would never be serious about me, and I think, at some level, I also recognized that he might be my downfall. Therefore, I never asked for anything more than casual encounters once I had left Jed. Despite all this, I was infatuated with Les.

I first met him when I was about twenty-one years old, at a festival in Byron Bay. He struck me as incredibly attractive, with his sun-tanned skin and sun-bleached long blonde hair from countless hours of surfing. He was cheeky, fun-loving, and enigmatic. At the time, he was high and dealing drugs, although I was not aware of this. I hadn't used heroin at this stage of my life, but he had. Looking back, I believe this was part of the allure, albeit on a subconscious level. I remember thinking, 'One day, I'll be close to this guy'. We had met through a mutual friend who had grown up in the same neighbourhood as him.

4

My First Habit

I was twenty-seven years old. Jed and I had been living together now for almost two years. I had been using heroin most days for about three months. I was shooting up mostly on my own. My friend Anna would often meet me at work during lunch time and we would go score together and hit up in the car at the closest park. She would then drop me back to work. I always bought a decent amount to keep me going for a week or so. I was using up my savings quickly and towards the end of that three months was using every day. All of this was done in secrecy. Jed had no idea I hid it that well. That is a part of addiction, you hide it from the very people who are right in front of you. And you kid yourself that you have things under control. At the end of a fourteen-day stint without a break, I woke up in a sweat next to Jed. It was my pay day at work and Jed knew this. I was in unfamiliar territory; I had never had a physical dependence to heroin, and it caught me off guard. I could not think clearly, I was feeling sick, my whole body was jittery and shaking and I felt crazy. I was sick with the fear of Jed finding out on top of things. I said I wasn't going to work, and he said he would go and pick up my pay. He said he needed it for the rent. I phoned work and let them know he was coming in. I still had a little money left in my savings account of which he had no knowledge of. Jed returned home about an hour later, mortified that he had spent my whole pay in a half hour stint at the TAB. It turned out we had not paid our rent for the past couple of months. We had been doing a direct deposit into the owner's account and I guess that is why the real estate agents had not been in touch. Jed confessed that he had been gambling it all away as I gave it to him. This was back in the day when you actually physically went into the bank to make a deposit. I thought this is the moment to come clean about my own addiction. I was hanging out, my body now dependent on the drug and I needed a fix. I was also looking for some form of support or help in my confession to Jed, but he just exploded in a fury. He started to physically hurt me, which he had done in the past, but this was the last time. It was wintertime and I had a big coat on, plus I was shivering from the cold sweats of withdrawal from heroin. I saw my moment, grabbed my bag, and raced down the front stairs. He caught the back of my coat as I was halfway down the stairs. I slipped my arms out of the coat and clutching my bag ran as fast as I could next door. Our neighbours were home and I raced inside their house and hid, telling them I would explain what was happening. It all happened so quickly that Jed had not seen where I had gone. I peeked out the window to see him storm up the street. I was shaking with fear, compounded with the fact that I was withdrawing. I knew that it was not safe for me to go back home, and I knew that I needed help to get back on track so I phoned my parents from my neighbour's place (these were the days when most people did not own a mobile phone, when there were phone boxes on every second street corner and everyone had a landline). I told Mum that I would explain everything when I got there but could they come and pick me up from Red Hill. That was where Les lived, and I was going to have one last hit of heroin before confessing to Mum and Dad. I called a cab and was able to wait at my neighbour's place until it arrived. I didn't know what Jed was capable of if he caught me again at that moment. I never went back to that house again and the next time I saw Jed was at a friend's wedding a couple of years later when I was on day-leave from a live-in rehab. He tried to speak to me, but I just walked away. He no longer had any power over me.

It was around two in the afternoon on the day I had escaped Jed. I was at Les's place, and I saw my father arrive out the front of the house. I was high. I had purchased enough heroin to last me a few days. I had about a quarter of a gram. Back in those days, I could use about a third of that and get high. It was pure gear, not cut with a whole lot of filler like some of the stuff I would resort to in later years. I jumped into the car. I was high now, so I was no longer withdrawing. My body and mind had calmed, and I was feeling in control. I said to Dad that I would let him know what was happening when we were home, and I could tell him and Mum at the same time. I knew this was going to be a big shock to them and I knew I needed their help to change my course of direction. I clearly remember every visual detail of the moment I told them. We were seated at the dining table, and I just came right out with it. I am addicted to heroin, and I need help. They both burst into tears from the shock. They had no idea. Nobody did, except for me. I remember also saying, "Oh and by the way I smoke dope and cigarettes as well." I was twenty-seven and had never told my parents I smoked cigarettes, let alone everything else I was into. They had thought I was a health addict not a junkie!

Mum and Dad opened their arms and met me with pure heart. We became a team to get me back on track. I made an appointment with a local doctor in Indooroopilly. He prescribed some Valium and clonidine hydrochloride. The clonidine really helped with suppressing the symptoms associated with the opiate withdrawal. I was continuing to smoke marijuana. This was my first home detox from heroin. I still had the rest of the stash of heroin, and I managed to not touch it for the whole detox. I got a doctor's certificate to take two weeks off work. Being my first detox, I bounced back quickly. Within a week, I was starting to feel better. I recall my parents taking me to the botanical gardens nearby and that I was only able to walk a little way. By the end of the second week, I was back to full strength and back at work. My father and a close male friend of the family had gone around to my last house and gathered all my belongings and we put them into storage. I had been concerned about Jed's mental state and that he may be aggressive towards Dad but outnumbered he kept his distance. We left the house owing quite a lot of money, so we didn't see our bond back and gathered a black mark against our names for any future rentals. This must have an expiration date as I was able to rent my own place ten years or so later. Jed had owed me a couple of thousand dollars for a car he bought, and I contacted his father to retrieve that debt. I never spoke to Jed again.

5

My First Steps in Recovery

I touched base with a local drug and alcohol counsellor through a referral from the doctor who had helped me with the home detox. She was based in Indooroopilly Shopping Town, and I also started getting acupuncture in the same shopping centre to help with addiction to opiates. As soon as I was back at work and through my first detox, I started using heroin again. After all, I did have that stash tucked away ready to go. I continued to have weekly sessions with my counsellor and saw a psychiatrist for a few months once a week. I had no car but would borrow my parents' car to visit friends, score dope, and go to all of my appointments. It was only a matter of months before I had a habit again. My parents knew however all they could do was give me shelter and watch as I deteriorated before their eyes. They did express their concern; however, I was in the grips of addiction and much as I was going through all of the motions of turning up to all of my counselling and acupuncture appointments, I never imagined a life without heroin. Each morning, the first thing I would do is jump in the shower and have a hit in the bathroom. My dad later shared with me that as he dropped me at the train station for work each day, I would be stumbling to catch the train, barely able to walk as I was so high. He would wonder if today was the day I would come home without a job, having been fired.

6

It's Time for Rehab

Once at work, I would continue to self-medicate throughout the day. I was shooting up in the toilet several times a day. My habit was starting to rage. I had lost a lot of weight, weighing in at about 43 kg. My bones were showing in all areas of my body. I was very tired, and I could not think. I was barely managing to do my job. In fact, I had to lie down many days at work because I was so high. I had been working for Fiona for several years and had become manager of the company and so for this reason I believe I was given a lot of slack. I found out later from another staff member that Fiona had thought that I had an eating disorder. One day, her partner Patrick who also worked in the business found me asleep at my computer desk. I had nodded off at the keyboard. He told me to go home and the next day I resigned. I knew that getting the sack was around the corner and it was time for me to consider another option for recovery.

My drug and alcohol counsellor had told me about a 'live in' rehabilitation centre just outside of Logan. I had been reluctant to take this drastic action in the past; however, there were no other doors to walk through at the time. I did not want to go on the methadone program believing that if I did, I would be on it for the rest of my life. So, I filed an application which was accepted. It was a nine-month program, and you were not able to leave the grounds except for supervised day-leave several times throughout that nine-month period. I had to live there for two solid months before I could have contact with anyone outside the centre, apart from mail, which was checked before being handed to me. It was like living in a prison environment without the bars. You could leave at any time that you wanted but that meant you were leaving the program.

I wanted to be clean entering into rehab as I did not fancy climbing the walls without any marijuana, Valium and clonidine to take the edge off. I knew that I would be feeling uncomfortable withdrawing from pot but that was nothing compared to heroin withdrawal. I went to the local doctor and persuaded him to prescribe me the Valium and clonidine one last time. He confirmed with my drug and alcohol counsellor that I was booked to go to rehab and said this was the last time he would do this for me. I did end up going back to that doctor a year and a half later seeking more Valium and he was true to his word. He never prescribed it to me again or any other doctor for that matter.

Mum and Dad drove me out to the rehab centre on the day I was to start there. As they drove away, I had a mixture of feelings arising, mostly fear. I had spent my high school years in boarding school in Indooroopilly as Mum and Dad were in Papua New Guinea at the time and this triggered the feelings of overwhelm I had felt back when I was dropped off at boarding school for the first-time, watching Mum and Dad drive away. That was one of the saddest days of my life. I was, however, able to reason that I was now an adult, and I knew I did not have any other options at this point if I wanted to change my circumstances.

Upon entry, I was assigned a 'buddy' with whom I had to stay for the next month. She did not leave my side except for showering, going to the toilet, and sleeping. In fact, she even shared the same room with me. A buddy was another resident who had been there for a couple of months or more. Her name was Bec. Bec, along with another resident searched all my belongings and then performed a strip search on me upon my arrival. This was the way they stopped any drugs coming onto the property. As a part of the program, you were required to provide a clean urine test every couple of weeks. You were immediately discharged if any drugs were present at testing. Random urine tests were also administered to prevent drug use amongst the residents. Although I had been very homesick when I was a child at boarding school, I feel it had prepared me for this experience as an adult. Sharing a room with two other women, living in a community, and having a routine that everyone was to follow lest there were consequences were familiar to me. The rehab was set up in a way that it was run by the residents and overseen by several staff members. The longer you were there, the more responsibility you got. This was part of the program. The trouble is you have a whole lot of addicts living together with a number from jail getting a little more freedom in rehab as part of their parole. There was a lot of misuse of power by various residents. Developing routine was a prime objective of the program and the days were very structured. Sport was at six in the morning Monday to Saturday with a day off on Sunday. If you had any consequences to work off, you had to get up ready to start work at five in the morning for an hour. Sport is a word used rather loosely as you had the option of choosing to play tennis (only one court), volleyball, or walking the driveway. Most of us chose walking the driveway and it was taken at an 'amble' along with a chinwag. We were not meant to 'neg Rave' at all. This meant that any conversation we had amongst each other must not highlight the fun of taking drugs. Anyone could clock you a consequence if you did and believe me there were people ready to pounce and exercise their power at any opportunity. So, we skirted the fringes of this rule. I mean, when you have a whole lot of drug users living together what else are they going to talk about? The driveway walk was abandoned not long after I started out there. A staff member put an end to it as he caught us all dawdling down there one morning. Volleyball or tennis were the only options from that point on.

After morning sport, we had a shared breakfast. Then throughout the day, we had chores to do and groups to attend. We also shared lunch and dinner together every day. We did chores in different areas and rotated each month to gain some experience in working different jobs. In each area, you started at the bottom and worked your way up over time, much like any job out in the 'real world'. For example, in the kitchen, you started as a dish pig and graduated some months later into head chef, making menus and shopping for all the ingredients to feed all who were there. There were about thirty residents in total at any one time. Many did not make it through to the nine-month mark. Of those who did, most ended up relapsing. What rehab did offer was a period of abstinence and some structure. There were a lot of unstable people there. There were separate houses for the men and women. Men outnumbered women two to one. The women were housed in the middle house. There was a lot of 'sleeping together' going on which was against the rules and there were people there who did use drugs, but I kept my head down, stayed clean, and applied myself as best I could. Most of the consequences dished out by other residents were for things such as getting up and leaving your cigarettes on the table without making someone aware of them! Yes, it was a rule implemented to help you become aware of your belongings at all times and not leave things lying around. Other consequences were usually dished out by the people in housekeeping who were in charge of checking the cleanliness of the villas. Everyone had an area to clean within each villa and maintain for a week and then we rotated on to the next chore. Some really took this housekeeping responsibility to the next level, serving a consequence for one mark found in the shower and so on. Hence, most of us found ourselves up and ready to start work at five for an hour each day.

I was happy to see the end of my buddying days with Bec. She had been cruel to me most days, belittling me in front of others and just being downright rude and cold in her use of power. I took some of what she said and did to heart but mostly brushed it off. After all, I had another eight months to go! I was committed to see the whole program through from the first day and this worked to my advantage. I saw it through. I gained close to nine months of sobriety. I gained weight and got my health back. I was still smoking cigarettes, but they were the least of my worries. The last month of the program is spent at a halfway house, which is about a fifteen-minute drive from the centre. A meeting is held once a week in the city at a church, which you are required to attend as part of the program. You begin to attend this meeting a month before you get to the halfway house. The meeting is chaired by a staff member. At the time I was in rehab, many of the staff members were ex-addicts who had studied psychology or counselling and had gone on to work in the field. Most of them still smoked cigarettes! Once you have been an addict, it takes an enormous amount of dedication and will to become completely drug free. Anyone who had been through the program could attend the meeting as an ongoing support.

By the end of the first week at the halfway house, I had hooked up with another male resident who was staying there at the same time I was. We caught the train in together to go to the support meeting and on the train ride we decided to score and use that night. I knew of someone who lived around the corner of the church who sold heroin. We rocked up there before the meeting and scored some gear. We bought a fifty-dollar packet to share. Neither of us had used in about nine months so we no longer had a build-up of the drug in our systems. We would not need much to get high. We were also able to manage holding on to the packet until we got back to the house before hitting up. By the time we got home we were very excited, and then very high. From that day, we started sleeping together and proceeded to become more and more entangled with each other. His name was Gary. He was funny, sporty, and an extravert. The common thread was that we both wanted to check out of being accountable for our choices and actions in life. We both loved heroin and we both wanted to continue to use it even though we knew it was not sustainable. We were back in the cycle, and we were in it together.

By the end of the fourth and last week in the halfway house (we were the only two living there at the time), we both had a habit. I had been travelling to Brisbane to pick up more and more heroin until we were buying larger quantities and subsequently using daily. We used every day of the last week and then I had to do a last sleepover at the centre. The following day was graduation day. I gave a speech for a fellow resident. I had track marks on my arms, which I was hiding with long sleeves on a hot summer's day. I had not had any sleep the night before and had been climbing the walls with withdrawal but was able to manage myself to get through the graduation. Talk about double standards! It was a prime example of me not taking responsibility for myself and my own actions and a lack of transparency. In the time that I had spent at rehab, I had become more corrupt. It is true that the people you surround yourself with impact you greatly and I had just spent a year living with a bunch of people who had run on the wrong side of the law far deeper than any of my prior circle of friends.

7

Living with Gary

While living in the halfway house, Gary and I decided to move in together. We had found our new group of friends. We both hung out with other people from the program. Gary had started working with a husband of one of our peers in the program. When he went to work, I often went to her place for company. We found a rundown flat in Auchenflower to rent. We were renting directly from the owner, so we didn't need any references. Also, there was no cross-check on any prior rentals like they do when you go through a real estate agent. We didn't have much stuff. Mum and Dad gave us a couple of chairs and I had a few boxes with kitchen items. There was a bed already in the flat. The walls were paper thin, and you could hear the guy next door playing computer games until late in the night. There were two rooms, a bedroom with bathroom and combined lounge/kitchen. There was a shared downstairs laundry. There were no trees. It was surrounded by brown lawn and situated on a very busy main road. The rent was cheap and so was the flat. There was nothing welcoming about the space. It was fitting for a drug den! Gary and I were using heroin there from day one. We started using only at night as Gary had to go to work. As far as I know, he wasn't using before work. I was at home alone a lot and felt very lonely and isolated as I had no car and was disconnected from my prior circle of friends. I had no job and was having little to do with my parents because of the shame I was feeling about my failure to stop using heroin. I didn't want them knowing that I was using again. I just wanted to hide away in a fantasy world with Gary and be consistently high. Some days I went and spent the day with other people I had gone through the program with. We would score heroin and use together, sometimes at their place, other times at our place.

I started using during the day without Gary and he started to secretly score and use. I was using all of my dole check on heroin and he was spending his wage on it. We were stealing and hocking items of value for cash to buy gear with. I had managed to find a doctor to prescribe me some temazepam. It was a sleeping tablet in a capsule form back in those days (they later made it into a tablet probably because so many addicts were shooting it up). And that is what we were doing. We started shooting up all sorts of things. Liquid Valium, morphine, crushed-up Mogadon and crushed-up Valium. Basically, any downers that we could get our hands on went into our veins. I was sneaking into our stash during the day and Gary was pretending to put gear in my syringe when he was only putting water in it. We were looking out for ourselves only and we were both drowning. It was around Christmas time, and we had been living together for a couple of months when his parents invited us down south. On that trip, I managed to convince both his parents and his brother separately to lend us some money and we went and scored. When they found out what we had done they never spoke to me again. Gary had already taken them to their limits. I was starting to feel sicker and sicker, throwing up more and more so I went to the doctor. It never occurred to me that I could be pregnant! I immediately decided to have an abortion and reached out to my parents yet again for their help to pay for it and to seek their support in what was a very emotional time for me. There was never a question of keeping the baby. I had a heroin dependency, and I knew that Gary and I would not be able to provide a safe space for the baby. I knew I was not capable of being a mum in the way that my baby would need me to be. This did break me on the inside, but I just kept shooting up gear to mask my feelings.

On the day of the abortion, Mum came with me. There were quite a few other women waiting in line. There were limited options back in those days for an abortion. You could only have it done privately, and it cost a substantial amount of money. There was a wait of about two hours and then it was all over rather quickly. I was numb from the morphine they had administered for the pain.

That night, I went out with Gary, and we scored some heroin and used it. He insisted on taking more than half due to the morphine I had received earlier. We were always arguing over our supply, each of us desperate for the drug. It was my contact we had used to score, and after acquiring the gear, we drove around the corner. He pulled over and refused to share any with me. He injected the entire amount in one go and overdosed right in front of me.

I leapt out of the car and flagged down a vehicle that had just turned onto the street. The driver, who knew CPR, helped me drag Gary out of the car and managed to resuscitate him. As luck would have it, we were parked right in front of her house. She quickly ran inside to call an ambulance—this was back in the days before we all carried mobile phones. I was twenty-seven years old at the time. Gary survived, but it was a very close call.

In the subsequent weeks, I would spend my days at my parents' house. Dad would ferry me back and forth. One day, after living together for a few months, I returned to find that Gary had packed all his belongings into his car and left without saying a word. We never spoke again. His departure left me heartbroken.

I moved back in with my parents, but I couldn't stop using. I decided to return to the live-in rehab facility in Logan, about four months after my graduation.

8

Second Stint at Rehab

I knew the drill. It was an opportunity to get some routine back in my life and gain some clean time. I lasted three months before I left with yet another man, George. I convinced him to leave with me to go and score heroin. It had been a lot more difficult for me to settle into life at rehab the second time around. I had gone in with a physical dependency to Valium and temazepam and this took a lot longer to clear from my system than the heroin did. I was still feeling uncomfortable at three months and was looking for an escape. I also wanted a partner in crime. George and I checked out and got a lift to the train station. Within a couple of hours, we had made it into the city and I had scored some heroin for us. We stayed at my friend's place that first night and kissed and slept together for the first time. It felt awkward and there was no connection. We both felt it, but we didn't talk about it. My friend kicked us out the next day. He was happy for me to stay but not George. We rocked up at my old friend Les's. He said we could sleep in the corner of the lounge room on the floor. We scored some heroin from him and spent three nights there getting high every day. We both ran out of money and had nowhere to go. Les said we needed to leave. I had to call my parents for help, but I knew they would not be helping George as well. George decided to go back to rehab.

9

Diving Into the Abyss

Dad came and picked me up yet again from Les's. I was just not able to get myself on track. All I could think about was heroin. It was all I wanted to do. I just wanted to escape the world and enter my own little private wonderland, cocooned in a cloud of heroin. I spent my social security payment each fortnight on heroin, and I was stealing from Mum and Dad's wallets when I could. I hocked whatever I could for money for heroin. I was shoplifting and hocking those items for money. I was sleeping with men in exchange for drugs. The shame I felt was consuming me and I was desperate to escape from myself and my life. I just wanted to be high, I loved being high, nothing mattered when I was high, no-one could reach me, I didn't care what anyone thought of me, I didn't care full-stop when I was high. I chose being high because it felt good. I kept choosing heroin until it was about living or dying and it was only then that I realized that I could not do it anymore. It was only then that I really had another choice. Up until that moment, all I had seen was heroin and getting high. When faced with the fact that I would die very soon if I kept choosing heroin, I saw there was another choice.

The choice to live. Followed by the question, 'What decisions should I make in order to turn that into my reality?' At the time, I was mixing a lot of heroin with Valium and temazepam along with smoking a lot of dope and out partying every second night on speed, ice or cocaine and then using heroin to come down. The only thing I really wanted to use was heroin, but this was a way of stretching it out. I had racked up credit with several heroin dealers around Brisbane. I was building a tolerance to the drug and needed more and more of it to get high and then to sustain the high. As I killed off the opiate receptors in my brain, I just was not getting the same sort of high that I experienced when I first started out. Plus, I had taken all my friendships to the edge borrowing money to pay for a hit without ever repaying the debt. People simply did not want to be around me because I was incoherent with the cocktail of drugs I was consuming. I was disconnected from myself. I was utterly lost and simply not able to connect with anyone. This went on for a few months until I found myself behind the wheel of my parents' car with Dad sprawled across the bonnet. That was my lowest point and that was the day my life started going in the opposite direction. Back up out of the big hole I had dug for myself. I had signed up for the methadone program and I was to turn up at the West End Clinic the following day. This would be where I collected my dose of methadone each day. They administered a dose there on the spot to carry me through the night. Dad came and picked me up from Biala and took me home. It was the chance for a new beginning again. It has been a long journey to get to where we are now as a family some twenty-plus years later. We would not be thriving like we are in relationship to each other if we had not all been prepared to walk it together.

10

Getting Stable with Methadone

I was on the methadone program for about two years before I was given the opportunity to be a part of a trial through the Royal Brisbane Hospital to go through a rapid opiate detox using Naltrexone.

Methadone gave me the opportunity to breathe, to get some routine and stability in my life. I had to travel to West End each day to be administered my dose. After a few months, they transferred me to a pharmacy closer to home. There was a little more flexibility with this as you went to pick up Monday to Friday and then were given your weekend dose to take home with you. There was a stigma around being on methadone. You were considered a junkie, a lowlife by a large majority of the population. I felt a lot of shame about who I had become. Still, it was the only way forward for me and I had decided to live.

At this point, I was still using heroin every couple of weeks, but I managed to control it, relying on methadone to help me get through the interim periods. This allowed me to function in society without resorting to drastic behaviour to sustain an addiction. I was still feeding the addiction with an opiate, but it was a controlled dosage administered by a pharmacist. I continued my weekly sessions with a drug and alcohol counsellor and began to look for work. Concurrently, I was working on rebuilding my relationships with my parents and my friends who didn't use heroin. I severed contact with everyone I had met in rehab. I still saw Les occasionally and would use heroin with him, inevitably ending up sleeping together each time. I was not yet ready to sever that connection.

I met up with Elle every few weeks for dinner and some pot smoking, but we had ceased using heroin together. From time to time, I still used heroin with Anna. I enjoyed clubbing with friends, drinking copious amounts of alcohol, and using speed or ecstasy every couple of weeks. I continued my daily marijuana habit.

Eventually, I put together a resume and applied for hundreds of jobs, resulting in a single interview that didn't lead to a job offer. I began to walk each day for exercise and returned to getting weekly acupuncture treatments. I ate three regular meals a day, incorporating a variety of fruits and vegetables, and started gaining weight, moving from a frail 42 kg to a healthier 49 kg. Although I was still petite, at least my bones were no longer visible.

I developed a daily routine, waking up around seven and going to bed before ten, starting to feel more stable and settled. I began to assist more at home with cooking and cleaning and even helped my parents with their home-based business.

At the age of thirty, my drug and alcohol counsellor suggested I participate in a trial with the Royal Brisbane

Hospital using Naltrexone for heroin addicts. Over the past six months, I had gradually reduced my methadone dosage from 70 mg a day to 48 mg per day. This level was low enough for me to undergo a rapid opiate detox using Naltrexone under general anaesthesia in a hospital setting. I also completed a psychiatric assessment and had been stable on methadone long enough to be considered. I was one of two people selected for the trial. The funding was limited, allowing only two methadone users to go through the rapid detox, and the ideal candidates were those most likely to remain in the program for the full six months. I was progressing well and had a strong support system in place with my parents, a requisite for the trial. One parent had to commit to administering the Naltrexone daily and supervising the intake of the tablet. My father volunteered for the task.

11

The Naltrexone Period

The week before I was admitted to the Royal Brisbane Hospital for the rapid detox using Naltrexone, I used a quarter of a gram of heroin over a couple of days. I was also taking 48 mg of methadone daily. I got the gear through Les and we shot up together in the park. I was having a 'goodbye' moment. Goodbye to my favourite thing to do at the time. Goodbye to shooting up heroin and hanging out with Les. The heroin was barely registering these days in my body from years of using the drug and being on methadone, but I still got a little buzz from it. I still loved the ritual of it, and I still had a thing for Les.

Dad dropped me off at the hospital a couple of days later. I was to stay five nights in total. I was to have the rapid detox on the third night. They needed to make sure that I had not taken any opiates for forty-eight hours before the procedure and the only way to do that was to monitor me in hospital. I had made it more difficult for myself by using heroin beforehand on top of the methadone. By the second night, I was experiencing the worst symptoms I ever had withdrawing from heroin. Thankfully, they had given me my own room because I was literally climbing the walls because I was in so much pain. I was pacing around and around my small room with a wild look in my eyes and I felt like a crazed wild beast. It took all my willpower to stay the course. I knew that I had no other option if I wanted to succeed so discharging myself did not even cross my mind. The staff who were monitoring me believed that I was not going to make it. I proved them wrong and in those few days I built a resilience and a strength that I had never had before in my life. I also 'supercharged' my will. These are the qualities that got me to where I am today.

I remember being taken by mini-bus to where the procedure would take place, which was in another section of the hospital. On the bus, I met the other person, David, who was taking part in the trial. Up until that point, they had kept us apart for obvious reasons! They didn't want us discharging together to use heroin. He was coming off a lower dose of methadone than me and had not used heroin in the week leading up to the detox. He had not experienced withdrawal to the same degree that I had. The next thing I remember, I was waking up after the procedure in a room. I have seen footage of a person doing a rapid detox with Naltrexone and it was not pretty! Someone was at my side as soon as I woke up. I felt exhausted on waking up and after a few hours of observation, they piled us back in the mini-bus to return to the detox unit. It was about eight in the evening, and we had left earlier that morning for the procedure. David and I stepped outside for a cigarette. This was the first cigarette I had smoked in three days. The hospital had put nicotine patches on our arms to keep the nicotine withdrawals at bay as we were not able to smoke leading up to the procedure. My head reeled on the first inhale and I almost fainted. I noticed I was still wearing the patch. We all had a laugh as I ripped it off. For some reason, I remember that moment very clearly. One of the counsellors from the rehab I had spent time in was there. He had been in the area and had heard about the trial and had come over to see how the rapid detox had gone. I remember him talking about how he still craved heroin and that he missed it and said that the craving would never go away. He talked about heroin being a lover that you needed time to grieve losing. And that every day you needed to make another choice if you wanted to be drug free. He said that craving heroin psychologically would always be a part of my life, it was certainly true for him. Such is the power of that drug. It took about twenty years for me to ditch the craving for good. So, it is possible!

For the next two days, I slept and grazed on my food at meal times. I still had my own room. I got to know David as we ate meals together and smoked cigarettes. We became friends in a very short time. We had a common bond and we kept in touch after we left the hospital. We would meet up and smoke marijuana together and chat about the 'good old days'. I continued to drop in and see Les although these days we were only smoking dope together. There was no point in me spending any money on heroin as the Naltrexone was a narcotic antagonist so I was not going to feel the heroin if I did use any. I did test this out and sure enough no high! After being on Naltrexone for a certain period of time, you may become more sensitive to lower doses of heroin hence once through the program I would only need a small amount of heroin to get high. Knowing that was my motivation to keep with the program. It was not that I wanted to go backwards, it was just that, as that counsellor had said, much as I wanted to move forward, I was simply not able to get heroin out of my mind. I continued to crave it with every cell of my being.

I had monthly appointments with the staff at the hospital to check on my progress. I took the tablet in front of my dad every day. By the third month, I was starting to regret being on the program. I was still thinking of using heroin every day and was not able to move past that. I tried to hide the tablet under my tongue or in the side of my mouth to prevent swallowing it. I only got away with that a couple of times before my father caught me in the act at which point his trust in me deteriorated even more. It really was a difficult time for both of us and I felt humiliated and embarrassed every day. He felt frustrated with me and was losing hope in me. He had to watch me physically take the tablet and would check every part of my mouth to make sure that I had swallowed it. I was not able to get away with it again and I was angry about it but I knew that I had to keep with the program if I wanted to live. At the same time, all I could think about was using heroin. At the end of the fourth month on Naltrexone, my parents and I moved to the Sunshine Coast to live.

I took the bus to Brisbane for the next appointment with the hospital. That was in the fifth month of the six-month trial. Two weeks before the six-month mark, I stopped taking the Naltrexone with some resistance from my parents. At that stage, I had started to see a psychologist through the Nambour Hospital Drug and Alcohol Rehabilitation Department. I was also attending various therapy and support groups run by the department. I was travelling less and less to Brisbane to catch up with friends. An old friend of mine relocated to the

Sunshine Coast. We had used heroin together occasionally in the past and he introduced me to a source of marijuana. This guy had a massive operation going on in containers and so I was able to purchase pot at a very cheap price for a year or so before he was busted and went to jail. Because the pot was so cheap, I was able to smoke a lot and was able to afford it on my social security payments.

12

My Second Stint on Methadone

About six months later, I found myself back on the methadone program, this time through Nambour Hospital. Les, after going cold turkey and heavily relying on marijuana, used the money from his heroin dealings to travel overseas in search of a different life.

During that period, I had become close with one of Les's friends, John, who was also a heroin dealer. I had developed feelings for John, although we never became intimate. Despite him having a girlfriend at the time, I often found myself flirting with him, to no avail.

Every fortnight when my social security cheque arrived, I would borrow my parents' car and drive down to spend the night, sometimes the whole weekend. During these visits, I would stay at either John's or David's place, and heroin was always involved. I can't recall the first time I used heroin after the Naltrexone program, but what I remember is how quickly my low tolerance for heroin built up, given my previous habit.

I would go on weekend benders, partying all night on ice, then use heroin to help me sleep. Gradually, I started to buy larger quantities of heroin on my trips to Brisbane, enough to last me a few days, and before long, I was physically dependent once again.

I returned to the methadone program, referred by my psychologist, starting on a very low dose. I had no intention of remaining on it for an extended period; I simply needed some breathing space. Once I was on methadone, I was able to stop using heroin.

This second time around, I was somewhat removed from the group of people with whom I used to use. I didn't know anyone on the Sunshine Coast who used heroin, and once on methadone, I managed to resist the urge to travel to Brisbane. I lost touch with David and Les was overseas. I also stopped calling and visiting John. During this period, I avoided any interaction with anyone who used heroin, even when I went to pick up my methadone. I knew that if I ever found a supply of heroin on the Coast, my days would be numbered.

I started on 20 mg of methadone and over a six-month period I weened myself right off it at 2 mg. There were little side effects. I did not feel any withdrawal, which kept me stable and able to develop a routine. I connected back with friends of mine who did not use heroin and started to develop healthy relationships. I started to work for my parents in the family business. I was working with them Monday to Friday and living with them. It was challenging for all of us, but it was what I needed to get back on my feet. I started spending time in the sun, going to the beach on weekends, and walking every morning at sunrise. I ate healthy food and started at the gym. I went to bed early. I found a massage therapist and started having weekly massages. I started to save money as I was not paying rent and not spending my money on heroin. I was off social security and earning a wage. I was getting healthy, fit, and strong from working out at the gym. I got off methadone and continued working and going to the gym every day. I was getting high on exercise and regular massages were helping to remove toxins caused by years of drug abuse. I stopped smoking dope. I even stopped smoking cigarettes. I stopped seeing my psychologist and I managed to rack up a couple of years of not using heroin or dope.

13

Partying in Thailand

When I was thirty-three, I took a trip to Thailand. My second overseas trip in my adult life apart from going back to visit my parents when they lived in Papua New Guinea. I spent Christmas 2001 there. I went with an old school friend of mine, Katherine, who had never used heroin but we used to party a lot together. She drank a lot and was pretty wild. I had remained in contact with Les via email. He was still overseas but was going to be in Thailand at the same time. We met on Koh Phangan, the island in the south that was famous for its full moon parties. Les stayed with me in my bungalow. Katherine was nearby in another bungalow and a good friend of ours was staying next to my bungalow. Our close little group grew to eight people. We met up every night for dinner in some local restaurant and then would head out to dance each night at different venues depending on the DJ playing.

Les introduced me to Thai Ecstasy, otherwise known as 'yaba'. He knew about it from his travels in India. Yaba means 'crazy medicine' in Thai. It does make you crazy! It is a combination of methamphetamine and caffeine. It's a little red pill that you heat up over alfoil and inhale the smoke. If you swallow the pill, you do not get the same sort of high. Who would have known! Thanks to Les, we all got the best value for money! I absolutely loved it. It gave you a rush, which took you straight to the dance floor and you didn't stop for hours. We were also swallowing European ecstasy, which was very strong. Katherine never took any pills, but she drank a lot. Some nights, we ate magic mushrooms and went out to parties in the jungle. We did this night after night for a month. The days were spent coming down lying on the beach and swimming. We smoked a lot of charis, which we managed to get from an Israeli who had smuggled it in from India. It is a marijuana resin, a lot stronger than any of the marijuana we could get in Thailand.

People from all over the world congregated there for a continuous, non-stop party. This was in the early days, when it was just starting. At that time, it was a more intimate event, with DJs from around the globe playing music until late the following morning. The gathering was small enough that you could meet most of the attendees. We stayed for one month before we all went our separate ways.

Thankfully, I had a return ticket to Brisbane; otherwise, I might not have made it back. I was mostly in a state of unconsciousness due to how high I was. Some nights, I was so drugged up that I couldn't even stand. I remember being at a dance party overlooking the ocean, with the sun rising, barely able to move as I was situated in a corner. I was so high that I found it amusing. Fortunately, I survived! I was lucky to have a group of friends looking out for me. We all looked out for each other. I cherished the feeling of being part of a close-knit group and loved the sense of belonging. I also enjoyed partying hard and being high every night.

By the end of that month, I had become addicted to yaba. The other group members didn't consume nearly as many drugs as I did. Whenever I get hooked on something, regardless of the drug, I take it to an extreme. Consequently, I ended up purchasing over-the-counter morphine to manage the withdrawal symptoms, something you can find in certain Thai pharmacies. I even found some heroin there, buying enough to last me a week. This was during my last week there. I was so wasted that I could barely see, so it's a miracle I found my way back home to Australia. By that time, I was very sick and had a terrible cough from inhaling so much yaba, but I had experienced the biggest party of my life. Eventually, I think my system began to shut down. I had lost a lot of weight again and was in a constant haze. I don't remember the flight home or even how I got to the airport, but upon arrival in Brisbane, I was searched for drugs. Thankfully, there were no unexpected discoveries in my bag! I had no intention of smuggling any drugs in.

14

Back on Methadone

On returning to the Sunshine Coast, I went straight back on methadone. I had developed a physical dependency to heroin once more and was reeling from that month of gluttony. It was difficult for me to settle back into life at home and the methadone took the edge off for me. I only stayed on it for about a month and was on a very low dose. This was enough time for me to find my feet and develop a routine once more. I was back at work with my parents and still living with them.

Les returned to Brisbane with his girlfriend. Katherine lived in Brisbane. I found myself in Brisbane most weekends in the first half of 2002. I would stay with Katherine and we would go out clubbing. Les would stay there as well. I started to get into speed after I met, and fell for, a speed dealer. He was a crazy bastard, but I was smitten. He was unpredictable, unreliable, handsome, and wild. It was a whirlwind romance, although I found out later that he had a girlfriend and someone else on the side. We started to use a bit of heroin together to come down after using speed the night before. I was having big weekends and then getting back up the coast for work on Monday morning. I was very tired and barely managing. That only went on for a few months. Then I started going down to Brisbane every second weekend or so just to meet up with Les. I would book a hotel room and we would meet there and use heroin together. I only ever bought enough heroin to last a couple of days so I never developed another physical dependence to the drug. We were sharing needles and I contracted hepatitis C from him. I didn't know it at the time.

A few months later, Les left to go back overseas to meet up with his girlfriend. I stopped using heroin and would only occasionally travel to Brisbane to visit Katherine. It was later that year when I went to an all-day dance event with her. I had a supply of ecstasy and gobbled them throughout the day. Katherine had gone home with her partner and after dancing all day and night I found myself outside a nightclub lying on a seat very late in the evening in Fortitude Valley not able to move. My system was shutting down. A bouncer called me a cab and somehow I managed to get out at the other end and make it up the stairs to Katherine's place.

I managed to drive home the next day, but my legs were cramping up and had tingles that just drove me up the wall. I was not well, so I went to the doctor and had some tests. It turned out my liver was shutting down. My markers were through the roof and I tested positive for hep-C. I went to see various specialists about my liver.

15

A New Chapter

Having being diagnosed with hepatitis C and being so unwell with it, I found myself pulling on my resources to focus on my health. I found an acupuncturist in Maroochydore who had knowledge of healing hep-C using Chinese herbs. I started weekly sessions with him. I immediately liked him and admired and respected him. He was a martial arts teacher as well and had learnt acupuncture in a traditional way from his martial arts teacher. He used to party in his youth and ride motorbikes. He had a wakeup call when he crashed his bike and lost the use of one of his arms. It was a big lesson for him.

When the student is ready the teacher appears. And this was the case with Bernard. He was an amazing acupuncturist. From his years of training in martial arts, he had developed a keen sense of Qi. He was strong in his presence yet humble. I looked forward to my weekly meetings with him and was fully committed to taking all of the herbs he prescribed and was drawn to the lifestyle that he was teaching and living. I did not miss an appointment for two years. I started off with weekly acupuncture sessions for the first six months, which then stretched out to once a fortnight. I continued to take Chinese herbs for the whole period. I stopped partying and travelling to Brisbane. I stopped smoking marijuana and even stopped smoking cigarettes for a short time. I started to feel good within myself and became healthy at 54 kg. I believe the reason that I did so well under Bernard's care was because I felt a connection to him. It also helped that he had been a bit wild when he was younger. He lived his life from a place of self-mastery and I was deeply longing for that experience myself. I became hooked on working at being the best version of myself.

I took all of his lifestyle advice on board. I read books on Chinese medicine and ate according to Chinese dietetics. I started to incorporate Qi Gong practices into my daily routine taught to me by Bernard. By the end of the two years, I had normal liver function results and I had cleared the virus. A small miracle.

16

Becoming More Independent

I was about thirty-six years old when I decided to move out of Mum and Dad's home. I was still working in the family business and was feeling very solid within myself. I was going to the gym each day and was healthy and fit. I was going to Brisbane every couple of months to party on ecstasy and very occasionally meeting up with John and using heroin. That was the last time I saw John until many years later. At that time, I had found a new group of friends, none of whom used heroin or needles. I became very close with a girl called Renae. We are still very close today. That was also the last time in my life that I caught up with Elle and Anna. I had gone to Brisbane to stay at Anna's place and we had used heroin together. Elle came over the next day to see me. I am not sure why we never got in contact with each other ever again. It just seemed like it was over between us all. There was no longer any connection of any sort. I was starting to change, and my friendships were beginning to reflect that change within me. My friendship with Renae was a pivotal one in my recovery. We adored each other and we really had each other's back. She is ten years younger than me and was a breath of fresh air in my life at the time. I was getting stronger and stronger within myself and was ready to take the next step.

I found an advertisement in the local paper for a room in a sharehouse in the town of Seaside near Coolum. The ad was placed by Erick, a music producer who had experimented with lots of drugs himself in his earlier years. The room was on the top floor of the house and I had the whole floor to myself with my own bathroom. Ah, freedom! It was so liberating to have my own space after living at my parents' place for so many years and a blessing for them to see me go. I never used heroin again until about 2011, when I was forty-four years old.

Erick and I became good friends. I did start smoking marijuana whilst living there again but I was able to keep it to night-time only, except on weekends. I also continued to periodically party using ecstasy and cocaine but it was always with friends and never on my own, which had been a pattern of mine in the past. I was able to keep my partying from spilling into my work week by this time. I lived with Erick as my housemate for two years and it was a healthy, stable environment for me to grow and find my feet in. Erick was a responsible, reliable upfront person and he was someone that I could trust. I started to learn how to manage money with paying rent and bills and shopping for groceries. It was like starting out all over again as an adult. I also had to keep my part of the house clean and contribute to the cleaning of the common areas. I was working full-time at the family business and this became a lot easier as we were not all living together as well. I saw a naturopath for a good year and worked on my health. I got up at dawn every morning and walked on the beach before getting ready to go to work. I can still remember how I felt as I walked out onto the beach each morning and was hit by the golden glow of the sun as it rose above the sea. It was such an exhilarating feeling and I felt so joyful from the experience. I was beginning to feel joy without drugs.

When I was thirty-eight, I moved into my first place on my own. It was a granny flat under an old wooden house in Alexandra Headland near the beach. It was a lot closer to work and it was all mine. No more sharing a kitchen or living space. It was small and run-down and when it rained there was a problem with mould, but it was the perfect next step for me. By this time, Renae had moved away up to North Queensland but I had made a few friends by then on the Sunshine Coast. I had a mixture of friends; some were pot smokers and others were health nuts who didn't even drink. It was healthy for me to have that cross-section of friends, but I struggled with marijuana at the time. I kept giving it up only to find myself not able to function without it. That space was not a healthy environment for me, even though it had been the next best step in my evolution. Getting my own place was key in my becoming more independent. The lady who lived upstairs had an abusive boyfriend, though, who was very loud, aggressive, and unpredictable. He beat her up more than once when I lived there, and I was scared of him. I had lived in that granny flat for almost a year when a little stand-alone one-bedroom house came up for rent back in the town of Seaside.

I could hear the waves from my bedroom at night in my new place being right by the ocean. I could smell the ocean. It was a very safe, nurturing space for me. I stopped smoking pot and cigarettes. I went walking on the beach every morning, greeting the morning sun once again. I started back with acupuncture. I found the five rhythms dance practice and began to drive to Brisbane weekly to attend. I loved to dance, and this was the perfect medicine for me. It was so healing for me to find a space to dance where no drugs and alcohol were allowed. I explored a lot of feelings and memories in that dance practice. It was a way of moving stuck emotions and stagnation in the body. I always felt amazing after each dance. I explored art therapy with the dance as well facilitated by the same teacher. I uncovered some pretty dark emotions and found movement to be the perfect antidote. I didn't feel the need to take drugs; I could just dance it out.

I tracked down a dance therapist and took some one-on-one sessions with her. Expressing myself through movement, I was able to touch emotions that I was not able to in my counselling sessions. She was also in Brisbane and she agreed to see me on a Saturday morning. I was with her for about six months. I was fully committed to my recovery by now and was prepared to jump all the hurdles. It was about an hour and a half drive there for a one-hour session. It was the same drive each week for the five rhythms dance on a Tuesday night.

For me, it was about finding the modality and the practitioner that resonated for me and then being prepared to put in the hours. I did that and I kept showing up for myself. I never missed an appointment. When I committed to something then I gave it my all and this has served me well in my recovery.

Around the age of forty, I started to explore meditation and went to a weekly guided meditation run by a lady who has helped me enormously over the years. I also started up

African drumming lessons and made my own djembe. I went to drumming classes weekly for about three years. I was mixing with a new group of people. People who did not take drugs or drink. People who practised meditation and yoga daily. I was beginning to explore my inner terrain with a new awareness. At this point in my life, I was living responsibly. I was not drinking or taking drugs. I would still occasionally think about using heroin or marijuana but did not act on those cravings. I think I partied on ecstasy about three times over three years. I felt so ashamed, dirty and toxic afterwards. Having become more aware of my inner world, I found that I was not enjoying drugs in the way that I used to. And in fact, I was starting to feel so good within myself that I was no longer feeling the desire to take drugs.

17

Changing Addictions

In my early forties, I explored art therapy and found an art therapist in Brisbane with whom I connected. She agreed to see me on a Saturday, and I travelled fortnightly to Brisbane to see her for a double session over the period of a couple of years. Again, I turned up for every appointment and was fully committed. We used various media, such as clay therapy, drawing, sand play, and acting. It was another dive into myself. I can confidently say that I have turned every stone over in my years of therapy and I have looked into every area of my life and myself and this has been a necessary part of my growth and transformation.

I also took to travelling, taking a three-month trip throughout Lao, Cambodia, and Vietnam. I went on two expeditions to Arizona doing a couple of retreats with Raelene who was my meditation teacher and mentor/coach. The work I have done with Raelene has spanned a good seventeen years. I would not have made it to where I am in life today without her help. She is someone that I deeply admire and respect. She is incredibly wise and big hearted. I am so blessed to have met her and worked with her and still to this day I have an appointment with her every six months or so to keep growing and expanding. With her help I have come to forgive myself completely. I have built an incredible relationship with my parents, I have discovered who I am, and I have learnt to love and respect myself.

I moved into a unit closer to work and was continuing to go to meditation weekly. My unit had a lovely view of the lake and was a step up from my previous place. I was occasionally still smoking cigarettes, buying a pouch of tobacco, smoking the whole thing and then giving up again. This went on until my trip to Thailand at the end of 2015.

In 2012, I heard about an ex-addict who was an acupuncturist in Brisbane. I was handed a book he had written. His name was Jost. I read the book from cover to cover without putting it down. I immediately wanted to work with this guy. I had used heroin again a couple of times that year as a result of running into John. When I ran into John early in 2012, it was on the Sunshine Coast. He had been up for the day. I was excited to see him and was immediately drawn into his world. My old crush on him was reignited as he flirted with me. It had been seven or eight years since I had used heroin. We had a coffee together and smoked a joint. It had been some years since I had smoked marijuana and I got very stoned. He wanted me to drive back to Brisbane with him on that day but I had to show up for work the next day. I knew that going to Brisbane would lead to me using heroin. He even popped his glove box to show me the heroin. I did not use any on that day, which was a reflection of how far I had come in my recovery. However, I started to think about using and that created a snowball effect, a step backward. I travelled to Brisbane the next couple of weekends to stay with John and use heroin and smoke a lot of dope. I bought a bag of marijuana off him and started smoking weed again at home. At the end of the second weekend, I was done. I walked away once again, this time before I developed a habit and before it interfered with my life.

A few months later, Les returned to Australia from overseas. He came to stay at my place a couple of times, and I went and visited him in Brisbane a few times. I managed to just smoke marijuana with him until the last couple of visits when I ended up using heroin with him. I still had feelings for him but I could see that he really was someone who would drag me under. At this point, I was able to also see just how sick he was and I was not attracted to him in the same way that I used to be. I knew that if I didn't want to end up losing myself once again to heroin, I had to say goodbye to this friendship forever.

Just before this, I had spent a week with Jost receiving acupuncture treatments and learning about qi. This included several one-on-one sessions with a tai chi instructor, a yoga instructor, discussions about diet, and coaching sessions with Jost. I was greatly inspired by Jost. He is a person who devotes an incredible amount of time to his personal practices. He shared a similar background to mine, having been a speed dealer, yet he was now steadfast and drug-free. He was robust and full of qi. He was planning a retreat in Bali in a few months, and I knew I had to be there. Once I made that commitment, I consciously decided to never see Les, John, or anyone else I had used heroin with again. That was a significant choice for me, and I never used heroin after that.

I went to Bali for the retreat, and something transformative happened there. I can't quite articulate what it was. We practiced yoga and two sessions of tai chi daily. Jost guided us through various self-development topics each day. We explored powerful personal routines that we could incorporate into our daily lives to encourage the free flow of qi through our meridians. I loved what I was learning and began feeling truly alive from all the practices we were doing. Furthermore, there was something magical about that part of Bali that helped me break through some outdated limiting beliefs I had about myself. I returned to that same centre in Bali three more times, each with a different leader.

Upon returning to Brisbane, I lost all my luggage, which served as a powerful metaphor for leaving all my baggage behind. On my second day back on the Sunshine Coast, I arranged my first one-on-one tai chi lesson with an instructor recommended by Jost. I saw him weekly for an hour of tai chi followed by an hour of acupuncture. I continued this for about three years. While I continued to struggle with cigarettes, it was my only vice during that time. I practiced a standing tai chi meditation for half an hour every day for those three years and practiced the form every other day for half an hour. I was dedicated to the practice and started to feel strength within myself. I was more confident than I'd ever been and thought less and less about drugs. I completed a 200-hour yoga instructor course in Brisbane and committed to a regular yoga practice, dedicating half an hour to an hour each day. I was now hooked on qi and ready to put in the hours. Despite working full-time, I managed to fit in an hour and a half each day for tai chi and yoga.

I decided to leave the family business and live overseas, either in Bali or Thailand, and find a job teaching yoga. Just before leaving, with my flights all booked, I went for a skin check. I had noticed a lesion on my leg that had been changing shape and growing more rapidly. It turned out to be a stage 3 melanoma. It was extremely aggressive, requiring immediate surgery. Fortunately, it had not spread to any other part of my body. It had been caught just in time. I had to postpone my departure for six months while my leg healed from the surgery (they removed about a quarter of my calf, a large area, to ensure they got all of it). It healed nicely, and I received a clean bill of health to leave towards the end of 2015.

18

Living in Thailand

Before going to Thailand, I spent six weeks in India. I was smoking tobacco at the time but that was all. I had bought about six pouches to take with me overseas and the plan was to stop smoking once I finished them all. I spent most of my time in India, specifically by the Ganges in North India. I would do two hours of yoga practice each day and swim in the Ganges. I visited ashrams and sat in meditation and prayer. I ate simply, mostly dahl, rice, and fruit.

Once in Thailand, I travelled to Kho Phangan. There was a yoga school there that I had heard of through a yoga teacher of mine and I planned to spend my days there. Ironically, this was the same island that I had partied so hard at many years earlier. The full moon parties were still going on but they were on the other side of the island and I never travelled there once in the year and a half that I lived there. My days of partying were over and I felt that with every cell of my being. The place that I had almost lost myself was the very place that I really came home to myself in.

I found a little house to rent which was surrounded by jungle not far from the yoga school I attended. I signed up for their level one course and then was with the school for the whole time that I was there. I had planned to teach but I found myself instead taking a deep dive into my own practice. I had a kitchen in my bungalow so I lived very simply buying fruit and vegetables at the local market and cooking my own meals. I was doing up to six hours a day of a mixture of yoga, meditation, and pranayama. At the school, you had the opportunity to go up levels learning more and more different meditation and breathing techniques as you progressed. The school taught a traditional hatha yoga using the mind to track the flow of energy. The amount of time you held each pose grew as you progressed up the levels. A year and a half later, I was holding an asana for twenty minutes before going to the next one. With the mind you focused on the chakra that was being activated with each asana.

I barely spoke to anyone in that time. I journalled every day. I did not socialise in the way that many did at the school. I was focused on becoming as clear as I could. Once my tobacco ran out, which was towards the end of my second month at the school, I smoked my very last cigarette. I have not looked back since. I did a lot of mind training at the time and it took a lot of will initially on my part to stay the course. In the same way that I never believed that I would have a day when I would not think about using heroin, I also believed that life just would not be as fun without tobacco. I undid those beliefs and I replaced them with new ones. Today when I see someone who is stoned or smoking, I feel repelled rather than attracted to it. I strengthened my mind with that yoga practice to a point where I now am not ruled by the mind, but rather I can use the mind constructively. My practices have allowed me to come into a place where I am mostly responding rather than reacting to the world around me. This training that I have done with the mind is serving me well today.

After a year and a half, I ran out of money and came back home to the Sunshine Coast. I had continued to stay in touch with Mum and Dad whilst I was in Thailand and I was deeply grateful that they took me back into the business and initially into their home until I once again found my own place. I had been so shattered over the years, so broken that I had really needed that time in solitude to fully come back to myself. In that time, I became able to enjoy solitude, a reflection of loving myself, knowing who I am and enjoying my own company. I learnt to meet my own needs in that time and not look for distractions or others to fill me up. I no longer desired to escape and so no longer felt the urge to seek out drugs to change the way that I was feeling. On reaching the end of my money after a year and a half of living life as a recluse, I was ready to return to Australia and start a new life.

19

No Turning Back

It was August 2017. I was forty-eight years old, five years since my last use of heroin and marijuana and over a year since my last cigarette. I had returned to work in the family business and found a unit within walking distance of work, facing a lake. I continued my yoga practice, dedicating an hour each day. I resumed attending a yoga class led by the teacher who had guided me to the school in Thailand where she had completed her teacher training. Through this class, I met a woman who rented out the lower part of her house through Airbnb. Seeking a more permanent home, I approached her about becoming a full-time tenant. The unit I was living in was not ideal. After viewing her place, I fell in love with it and moved in within a few weeks. It was a pole house in Alexandra Headland, close to the beach and surrounded by trees, offering a large space with two bedrooms.

Inspired by several sessions with Raelene, I was motivated to pursue further training. My background in bodywork, naturopathy, and Chinese medicine led me to a man named

Gwyn, whom I discovered through a flyer. Gwyn offered a nine-month bodywork training program called Zenthai Shiatsu.

About fifteen years earlier, I had seen Gwyn at the Peregian markets, where he and several practitioners were providing bodywork in a tent. Despite their friendly, fun-loving atmosphere, I felt too shy to book a treatment. In hindsight, I was just not ready for what Gwyn would later offer me as a teacher and mentor.

In December 2017, I enrolled in the prerequisite, a four-day workshop. The group comprised about thirty people, and our experiences weren't confined to learning a bodywork sequence. We also sang, shared meals, and played games together. This experience was as much about building community as learning a modality. While I felt overwhelmed and scared, I knew this was my path forward. Gwyn, a humble and beautiful human being, has a unique gift for drawing out the best in everyone. Under his guidance, I was driven to give my all. Although I didn't initially participate in all the activities, I pushed myself to try everything by the end of the three years I trained with him. By stretching my boundaries, facing my fears of failure, rejection, and judgment, I discovered that I was capable of more than I realized.

In 2018, I began the therapist training, a monthly four-day intensive. The course pushed me to my limits, but the growth I experienced prompted me to repeat it the following year. I loved the bodywork and Gwyn's unique style of yoga, called 'Zenthai Flow'. I attended his classes for about three years, finding a space where I could truly be myself. I flourished, making lasting friendships with people who are still part of my circle today. I traveled to Bali three times to attend Gwyn's teaching sessions and participated in two yoga and Ayurveda retreats, followed by the Zenthai Flow yoga teacher training.

That location in Bali held a significant place in my heart. Jasri, a quiet fishing village on the east coast of Bali, was far removed from the hustle and bustle. I had profound personal breakthroughs each time I visited. The place allowed me to be present and truly live in the moment. I have strong memories of the times I spent there on all four occasions. The nearby mountain added to the energy of the place. It was a place where I felt rooted, nourished, and energized, influenced by both the tangible and intangible elements of the area.

On my third visit there doing a yoga and ayurveda retreat, I managed to gather the confidence to participate in an expression session. This was towards the end of the second year that I had spent training with Gwyn. There was a lot of creative talent in both groups that I had gone through the training with and I felt very insecure about doing anything. I decided to do a dance in front of everyone. This was a huge decision for me. I was petrified at the thought of doing it but I knew I had to give this a go as the opportunity may never present itself again in my lifetime. I also knew that if I overcame this fear that was crippling me then who knew what might be possible for me. I will always vividly remember every detail of this moment in my life. I will always savour and cherish that experience. I stepped through so much fear just to get up in front of the group of about thirty people. I danced the first half of the song with my eyes closed and then when I felt brave enough, I opened my eyes to see all looking at me. I had nowhere to hide. My mind was telling me I looked stupid and ungraceful. It was telling me everyone was bored with what I was doing but there was another part of me, my spirit, that was absolutely soaring. I danced the whole song and it seemed to go on forever. The moment I opened my eyes, everyone cheered. I can still hear that applause. I wanted to crawl away and hide after I had completed the dance but what happened after that was that I felt loved for who I was. I felt OK to be me. And I got over myself. The shackles were gone. It is one of my favourite moments in my life and I gained so much from extending myself. I learnt that vulnerability is pure power and that as human beings if we are courageous enough to be vulnerable then we touch hearts. What a gift!

I started to live an ayurvedic lifestyle after learning about ayurveda. Living this way has helped me become healthy, balanced, and joyful. The Zenthai Flow yoga teacher training saw me step into my potential as a teacher and leader. Over the two years I spent under Gwyn's guidance, my confidence in myself grew and my heart opened and healed. I also had the privilege to live at Gwyn's property for three years where I blossomed. I had a granny flat there and shared the house with one of my closest friends and her partner. It was at the base of a very powerful mountain. I really found my feet in this space and felt loved and respected by all who shared the land there. This place was a healing vortex for me. It was in this space that I created the next big step in my growth and evolution. At this point in my life, I was able to socialize without thinking of drugs. There were people in the course who took drugs but I was never around when they did and I did not seek that experience out. I just was not interested in getting high anymore. I was having fun without any drugs being involved and the connections I was making, the confidence that was growing within me, being loved and accepted for who I was, being respected by others, these were all things that far outweighed any fleeting high that drugs provided.

A sense of stability and groundedness was progressively taking root within me. This transformation was achieved by consistently exploring supportive practices, prioritizing personal growth, seeking necessary help, showing up consistently, challenging myself to face fears, embracing vulnerability and authenticity, taking responsibility for my life, incorporating yoga and meditation into my daily routine, and learning to love and accept myself as I am. Each of these elements played a significant role in my successful recovery from drug addiction. They altered every aspect of my life, showcasing the cumulative power of these changes.

20

Addicted to Life

In March 2022, I became a homeowner. I purchased my first house with a lot of help from my now proud parents and a loan from the bank. I knew at this point in my life that I would never use heroin again and that I did not need to worry about slipping back into old ways. I absolutely love my home. I am so happy here. It is close to the beach. It is surrounded by greenery. It has a view. I even have my own pool. It has a Bali sort of feel to it and it is all mine. Everything is flourishing here, the plants and trees, the wildlife, the energy of the place and myself. I feel cherished and loved in the space. This is my sanctuary, my temple. I have never felt so good in my whole life. I continue to live an ayurvedic lifestyle and have many personal practices that nourish and support me. I have a daily meditation, yoga, and breathwork practice. I have close, connected friendships. I have a daily gratitude practice, which I share with my dear friend Renae. I have an incredible relationship with both of my parents with whom I still work. I feel full and happy. Taking drugs just does not cross my mind in the way that it used to. They no longer have any power over me. I reflect back to the conversation

I had with the counsellor from rehab during the Naltrexone trial where he talked about never really getting away from thinking of heroin, that it always lingered in the background. That is simply not my story. Honestly, when I look back on those times, I just do not recognize myself. It is difficult to believe that it was me. I am proof that you can move beyond the addiction. We become what we think. We create what we talk about. I prefer not to use labels such as 'I am an addict'. They seem so limiting. I chose to believe that I could get to a place in my life where I was standing in my own power and I have. It was not an overnight journey. It took me a good twenty-five years of consistently showing up for myself, many steps backwards as well as forwards until it became mostly steps forwards. I had to keep picking myself up and putting myself back together again. I kept asking for help and I kept putting in the work. It took a lot of work on my part to change thought patterns and to keep myself on the path. As a result, I am now leading my life from a place of self-love, self-respect, self-value, and self-acceptance. My choices and desires reflect that. I don't think about drugs unless I have a random dream about them or unless I am recounting some part of my past in conversation. I am not curious about using drugs anymore. What I am curious about, is how much more can I grow and stretch myself in this lifetime? How much can I love? How brightly can I shine? Another thing that I notice about myself is that I no longer want to be someone else, I no longer look at others and wish I was like them, wished that I had their life, their looks, their abilities and so on. Yes, I am inspired by others but that translates now into 'what can I do to be more of myself?' I know who I am, I am connected to myself, and I am able to love myself just as I am. That doesn't mean I stagnate. Every day, I strive for personal growth and evolution, working towards my ideal self. I've managed to effect change in every aspect of my life, moulding myself into the individual I am today. Over recent years, I've developed a website and produced a movie, both of which serve as platforms for sharing the lessons I've learned on my journey toward wholeness. Writing this book is another endeavour aimed at inspiring others to reach their full potential. I take pride in who I've become and remain eternally grateful to my beloved parents, who have accompanied me on this journey and continue to support me. To Mom and Dad, I express my profound love and gratitude. Thank you.

www.ingramcontent.com/pod-product-compliance
Lightning Source LLC
Chambersburg PA
CBHW070335120526
44590CB00017B/2889